THE FISH

— & —

THE DOVE

Mary-Kim Arnold

THE FISH
—— & ——
THE DOVE

Mary–Kim Arnold

Cover Photo: Xander Marro, "Arrows" [http://xandermarro.com/]
Book Cover Design: Steve Halle
Book Interior Design: Sarah Gzemski

Published by Noemi Press, Inc. A Nonprofit Literary Organization.
www.noemipress.org.

"These are the wars for which we have paid, from which we have benefitted, by which we are traumatized."
—Viet Thanh Nguyen

"All men, I think, have a favorite war."
—Farid Matuk

CONTENTS

SELF-PORTRAIT AS SEMIRAMIS

Had I been raised by doves
wouldn't I have learned
to fly

By wolves
to hunt in packs

Had I been raised by gods
wouldn't I too
be godlike

In the movies the orphan
is the killer
not loved enough
unwanted

But wasn't I
most
        wanted

My mother
fish goddess
dove into the sea
for the sin of loving
a mortal man

I love a mortal man too

At night I coax him
from sleep

rousing him
with my mouth

By day
we build high brick walls
around us
        our Babylon

Had my mother lived
to see me rise from this boundless
deep
        would she recognize me
as I have grown large
and my arms have become
the long arms of the sea
reaching over
                and over

                        for the shore

LEGACY

It was not my choice to skin rabbits

to let their blood

                              drain over me

This is something that nobles do   and I

am descended

                    from a long line of royalty

We fear no armies of men   Rabbit blood is warm and thin

I was fully clothed when I began the rabbit ritual

then disrobed in accordance with tradition

Rabbit slaughter naked in the dim light

white fur stained red   pale skin streaked red

red pools on the marble floors   I bathe in red

Did I mention that I am of the noble class

You probably have noticed this already

Wasn't I beautiful in my untouched youth

before I bled   but now my hands

my hair

         have you ever seen so much red

You see my father is ill   his heart is weak

I bring him tea   he does not drink

I mash ripe figs with a spoon

and press the thick paste to his lips

with the same spoon I gouge out

rabbit eyes and tell him   Father they are all blind now

I show him the spoon   their eyes   my hands

He nods his head beneath its heavy crown

My father's bed is the altar where we gather

all the blind rabbits and me

We know the men are advancing

We can hear them sharpening steel

When they reach us   I will throw myself naked

across the body of my dead father

and they will see us   and they will know

from what nobility

                we have descended

HISTORY

Dying, the prime minister said,

"If I could speak, you might understand,"

to which his killers replied:

"Dialogue is useless."

                        They took a taxicab

to turn themselves in. Eleven naval officers,

all barely twenty years old,

and the people love these men so dearly

that eleven severed fingers

arrive at the courthouse with a petition

to spare their young lives.

Youth favors action. The old

wish only to speak.

                        In my younger days,

I threw my soft-limbed body around

as if redemption were possible.

Now, time is a robe stitched through with ash

I keep trying to shake off.

Looking back, the path to war is clear

as an arrow whistling through still air,

but now at the courthouse

men smoking and taking photographs

as if their living eyes could see

what the dead already know.

                    The old judge scratches

his bald head as he approaches —

white straw hat

                    carried off by the wind.

OCCUPATION

During the occupation we all eat fruit

grown in poisoned earth

                          What is history if not the breath

of the damned rising up?

In this blurred photograph I pretend I can see

                                      my mother

so limp-limbed and worn   my father

                            raising his hand

against the blazing sun as if he could take it —

I no longer sleep at night   I no longer speak

my own name aloud

Every night a howling wind

shears the bark from trees   dismembers branches

Outside a stray cat caught in a steel trap

cries for hours

how long this dying takes

SILENCE

All the girls wore men's clothes
because they didn't want to get raped

All the girls did hard work
because the men were not around

All the girls slept in one bed
and shared one thin blanket

Do you know how cold the mountain is at night?

FORGOTTEN WAR

I.

No war is forgotten to those who lived through it.

I take a weekend away to write but spend whole days

watching war documentaries online.

Some are grainy amateurish affairs but I watch them anyway.

> *For the next ninety minutes, you'll see Korea*
> *the way the soldiers saw it—*
> *in full shocking color!*

On screen men are always marching

or refugees in white plod away from the burning city.

> *Civilians were a big problem*

Men marching in mud and then in snow

> *the most desolate country you ever wanted to see*

missiles hurtle toward the earth

then blow it open—

What am I searching for?

On screen, a crying baby in a wooden cart: This is not me.

Men held naked at gunpoint: This is not me.

Piles of corpses abandoned in a roadside ditch: Not me, not mine,

not my war and yet—

One must choose sides, it seems.

You are brave or you are the enemy

You stand and fight. You fight or die. You die fighting.

My mother was a child of this war. She blurs my vision.

Is it useful to ask

who is the enemy or where do I belong

useful to lay claim to someone else's suffering

to keep watching

this endless march

through mud and snow

through winter so cold it froze

the wounded as they fell

their arms raised and reaching

froze the blood so fast it wasn't

until later as they thawed

they bled out

Not useful

Not mine

Not now

Not while

all these bodies keep piling up

in my name.

II.

All the documentaries in the world
will not bring my mother back.

It's not bitterness if it's true.
This is a rule I just made up.

*

When the president abandoned the city
he left behind what he no longer needed
golf balls
oyster knives
gold-rimmed tea cups

wreckage for people to pick through

orphans who clogged the streets
were just another problem to solve
to clean up and ship out

and twenty years later still
sending their children away
and thirty years later
and forty

and here I am
still looking for signs
still looking for reasons
trying to freeze the frame to find
my mother looking out at me
from the ruins
my own face looking back.

III.

Was I the good Korean or the bad one?

"Honey, all cats are black in the dark,"
my American father would sometimes say, winking.

I thought we were talking about cats, but when
my American mother clucked her tongue at him at glared
I felt my whole body go hot then cold.

The bad Korean, for sure.

*

A devout childhood spent on my knees I feared
that at night a demon would possess me
so I would pray to the virgin mother to fill me
so full of grace that there would be no room left
anywhere in me
for anything else to enter.

*

Years later in the bar
when I didn't want
to do shots
with the loud laughing men
didn't want
to slide my barstool down
closer
looked away
when they patted their laps

and tilted their heads at me
didn't one of them ask me
what the fuck
my problem was
didn't one of them ask
don't you know
what we could do to you
didn't one of them say
you wouldn't even
be here
if we didn't go
over there and save you
don't you know
who we are
who you are.

*

One must choose sides, it seems.

That night, I spoke the names of saints aloud
remembered my old novenas
fell asleep to the sounds of my own fear.

Vigilance is one way
to keep my mother alive.

*

You are brave or you are
the enemy. You love it or
you leave it.
You stand and fight. You fight and die.
You die fighting.

*

You can stay up all night counting corpses
and still not know who you are.

You can open your mouth to speak
but still not know your own name.

NO GUN RI*

In the tunnel, babies were born then died.
Their whole lives a bright burst of gunfire
and the wailing of their mothers.

*

A baby (born and killed in the tunnel, posthumously named Park No-myong)
A baby (born and killed in the tunnel, posthumously named Cho Seung-yon)

*

0, 0, 1, 1, 1, 1, 1, 1, 1, 1, 1, 1, 1, 1, 2, 2, 2, 2, 2, 2, 2, 3, 3, 3, 3,
3, 3, 3, 4, 4, 4, 4, 5, 5, 6, 6, 7, 7, 7, 7, 8, 8, 9, 9, 9, 10, 11, 11, 11,
11, 13, 13, 13, 13, 13, 14, 14, 14, 14, 15, 15, 16, 16, 16, 16, 16,
17, 17, 17, 17, 17, 17, 18, 19, 20, 20, 20, 21, 21, 21, 21, 21, 22,
23, 23, 23, 23, 23, 26, 26, 27, 27, 27, 27, 28, 28, 28, 28, 29, 29,
30, 30, 30, 30, 32, 33, 34, 35, 35, 36, 36, 36, 36, 37, 38, 38, 38,
39, 39, 39, 39, 39, 41, 41, 41, 42, 42, 43, 43, 43, 43, 44, 44, 44,
45, 45, 45, 46, {my age would appear here}, 47, 47, 48, 48, 49,
50, 50, 50, 51, 52, 52, 53, 53, 54, 54, 55, 55, 55, 56, 57, 57, 57,
58, 59, 59, 60, 61, 61, 61, 63, 63, 63, 65, 66, 73, 76, 77, 85, 85

*

… finally and with a long sustained cry she delivered the child …

… toward the mother-in-law struck by a bullet …

… wounded at the wrist and could not carry …

… left the baby and the old woman behind and slipped out …

---

* The No Gun Ri massacre took place over three days, between July 26 and 29, 1950, in the early days of the Korean War. South Korean refugees, attempting to flee Seoul, were trapped and killed by U.S. military beneath a twin-underpass railroad bridge near the village of Nogeun-ri. The victims were mostly women and children.

DEMILITARIZED ZONE

what rises against the sky

steel-girded   cocksure

what slices the gray air

is government-sanctioned

the village is just a village

                              is just   is just

*

we take the bus to the border

the tour guide hands out forms

and we sign them   promising

not to point our cameras

in the wrong direction

see, here is how you will recognize what side you are on

see, here is how you will know where you belong

as if history's frayed threads aren't unraveling

as if the ground beneath us isn't bones and blood

*

who was taken during the war

whose small bones

who was not loyal enough

in the battle of whales

the backs of shrimp are broken

*

later   an armed guard boards our bus

and seizes our cameras

film in black ribbons unspooling at his feet

image of a woman's face

image of corded telephone and fax machine

image of an armed guard boarding our bus

*

the tour guide says they are only trying

to protect us   as we idle

on the Bridge of No Return

but we are not asking for much

what I mean is mother tongue and father country

what I mean is let us finish what they started

SELF-PORTRAIT AS KOREAN MOTHER

1.

The ruined villages we saw, the fields burned black.
When it rained, we could see ghost flames in the moonlight.

2.

We were already late. She was waiting when we arrived.
She gave me a train ticket back. She took my hand and patted it.
"Good girl. Now your life will begin again. Now go."

3.

Back home, half-moon suspended in mist.
At my feet, a white bird fallen, hardly bigger than a stone.

In dreams, you return to tell me
I am not trying hard enough. No distance greater
than this distance.

SELF-PORTRAIT AS PRAYING MANTIS
(ABANDONED KOREAN DAUGHTER)

Let my body emerge   from these dry brown husks

with black dots for eyes and voracious

mouth like fly paper   summer's dry heat

shedding skin

              does not rain for days   does not

give way   the Korean goddess of rainfall

is asleep in the north

The only woman who can tell me   about my mother

is six thousand miles away and dying

sends me letters on blue paper   so thin it is translucent

Hangul small and tight   yielding nothing

Nymphs are born by the hundreds

at birth they resemble adults

              who do I resemble?

From time to time I remember   St. Anthony patron saint

of lost things   the nuns teach us to invoke him

> *St. Anthony, St. Anthony please look around, something is lost*
> *and cannot be found*

Ask the woman for a name   for one word or two

that will describe my mother   but my letters come back

unanswered   years and years unanswered

years of looking for a name   to drape across

this cradle of time   name to stitch into

this swaddling blanket   name to burn into

this skin   this skin that must resemble her skin

From time to time I remember   sparrows bathing in dust

wild turkeys strutting through the dry brown yard

                                        inside the house

bowl of persimmons on low table   and a woman

hair falling down her back

                looking away

never turning to see   never turning back

never looking

for me

      St. Anthony patron saint of lost causes, please look around

In the garden they lay in wait   then strike

death grip on their unsuspecting prey   so fast

                           Oh mother

my method is ambush too   I will wait

for so long   will spend the days waiting

but then

        when you are close enough

I will come at you

     fast   and I will take you

     apart

HUNGER

I try to run away from home once.
I am going to find my real mother, I say,
the one who looks like me.

I pack a bag with toy plates and the five-dollar bill
that came tucked inside my birthday card
For a Special Girl Who Is Five Years Old.

I take the elevator to the top floor
of the red brick apartment building we call home
and start knocking on doors.

If anyone hears my small fist pounding
against the painted steel, they might look out their peepholes
but see nothing.

Maybe the hall light flickers. Maybe
a dog barks behind a door. Maybe I am hungry
and I have already gone so far.

When I come back my mother
has spread a blanket on the floor
and set a plate out with cheese sandwiches.

I thought we could have
a picnic she says. She pours ginger ale
and I swallow it.

AMERICAN GIRLHOOD

WHO
No one speaks of it directly. Once or twice when my mother appears to pick me up from school, someone would ask, "And who is she, to you?"

BOMB
I could be Chinese, like the restaurants, or Japanese, like the bomb. They look back at me blankly when I say the word Korean.

AFTER
Behind the Sadore Lane apartment complex, where the boys hang out after school. The first girl they invite is Janine. Then Theresa, then Val. By the end of that year, all my friends have gone. Debbie comes back with a bruise on her cheek. Mark doesn't come back to school after that.

KEY
Pocket sewn into the waistband of my uniform skirt.

COVER UP
I stay up late to watch the television show about fashion models who are also undercover spies. I watch broad-shouldered men prance and silk-draped women swoon.

RANCH
He leans against the coin machine in the arcade. Blond. Slim-hipped in straight-legged jeans. I spread a handful of bills and coins across the glass of the broken pinball machine.

My, my, my, he says. Will you look at that. I follow him out to
the warm night. The sky is filled with stars.

SLIPPERS
The summer everyone wears "Chinese slippers." Black cotton,
rubber base. Banded in bins at the Woolworth's. Or at the flea
market for five American dollars.

DREAM
Standing in a pool of thin yellow light, circled by doves I hear
car alarms in the distance. Doors closing then opening again.

GONE
My father packed his two good shirts and his old guitar.
Winked at me as he slipped out the front door.

SLEEPOVER
No one sleeps. Head to the floor, I am alert to vibrations in
the boards. I hear parents sighing in their bed. In the morning,
dust glistens. I watch for signs of life.

LAKE
High grass on our ankles. Ice cream cones wrapped in paper.
Lemonade from a red thermos. Iced tea from a yellow one.
Cold fried chicken we eat with our hands. The dock in the
middle of the lake is an island. I am afraid to get too close.

NEIGHBORS
There are reports of a cult roaming the village at night. After
mass, the parents whisper what they have heard. A pile of
stones in a church parking lot. The bones of small animals.
Dark sacrifices made while everyone sleeps.

FIRE

The night of the fire I stand barefoot on the sidewalk and watch smoke, thick and black, billow from the roof. Later we hear about the woman who left her stove on for hours. Then what is one match lit in darkness?

GEESE

The wide tree-lined path along the river. Highway close but its noise gentle like running water. My mother tears slices of day-old bread for the geese. Their tense expectant din.

PARADE

The intersection where as a child I watch the parade pass though. Trumpeter wilted and forlorn. The rouged girl waves her baton listlessly through the heavy air.

TRAFFIC

Dry grass beneath us. Rush of highway traffic alongside. I tell him his name means "you are beautiful" *en francais*. He places his hand on the waistband of my jeans. Lays it flat and leaves it there until I guide him in.

STORM

In the storm, rain soaks the windowsills and the hems of curtains. Potted violets left on the balcony overturned by morning. The backseat window cracked open, the seats drenched through.

SPONGE

Today contraceptive sponge in a pink square box on a high shelf beneath the glare of supermarket light. I decide not to rely on anyone but myself.

DONE

Moon slivered over the parking lot. It is done quickly. Crickets and far-off fireworks. In the morning, the cooing of doves.

SELF-PORTRAIT AS UNGRATEFUL
AMERICAN DAUGHTER

Don't quite know how to tell it. That we ate in silence. At the restaurant

near my dorm before my mother drove back home alone. That I

was glad to be rid of her. Having spent the long weekend with her

in the stifling air of the house I grew up in. Lying in bed that morning

listening to her tinny radio news as she put the dishes away. Then in silence

as she drove the four hours to bring me back to campus. Don't know how

to say that once she left, I got high with my friends.

That is what we did then. On our backs with music playing.

She made it home, but barely. The pain in her stomach

so bad she drove herself straight to the hospital. Her appendix. Burst.

Spilled its cancer out "very aggressive" and spread

through her abdomen. Don't know how to say I got the phone call

still high. Thought what the fuck is she calling me for,

now. But it wasn't her. It was her sister to tell me

that my mother was coming out of surgery and they thought it went ok.

That I hung up the phone and went back to my friends for a while

before I packed a bag for the train. She was home

for a few days before she had to go back.

"Very aggressive and very rare." Gelatinous tissue that spread

through her abdomen and made its way to her womb. So

rare it is called an "orphan" disease. This orphan lodged

in her belly. Grew there. Grew large.

That she called it *"l'enfant"* and patted it as she stood in the doorway

on one of the few afternoons she could stand in the doorway

and laugh a little. "*L'enfant terrible.*" Crowded everything out. Don't know

how to say that the surgery they wanted to do is called "debulking,"

a terrible word. Don't know how to talk about

the lurid frailty of the body, its horrible mass. It was too late

for debulking anyway, the cancer insinuated so deep

and *l'enfant* growing so big and so fast. Time was not

something I had thought we'd run out of. So many years

of silence. When we had stopped saying anything

of importance. When either we fought or cried. When we were tired.

When she was tired. When, in the end, I left. Abandoned her. I

had never really wanted another mother. Rejected her

as surely as the blue velvet coat she bought me

when I was a child. She had hung it on my bedroom door

and when I saw it marched into the kitchen with it, holding it out

and shaking my head. I wanted red. What I had wanted was red.

What she offered would never be what I wanted. It was the coat

and then it was other things. The way a grain of sand becomes

a stone. The way a stone becomes a mountain. The way a mountain

can stand against years of artillery fire, but wears

its scars across its face. In the end, you still have to choose.

COMFORT

I did not learn much
about history
on my back
pressed against the door
of his Japanese car
while the ghosts
of our ancestors
paced in the parking lot

Did not learn much
from his approach:
I know
your people
hate my people but you
are too pretty
to be left standing here
alone

That night
and nights after
it was not empire
we spoke of
not occupation in
our mouths

Years later
on a busy street
and then upstairs
he tried
to bring it all back

pinned me down
on my own floor

There are many ways
to remember
in a room
barely large enough
to lay
one tatami mat
down

IN THE CITY OF MEN

For a time I worked in a building adorned with the head of a man

let's call it the Man's Head Building

and everywhere in the building one could not escape the heads of men

Men in the elevators Men in the hallways Men in the café taking up chairs

Men carrying newspapers and briefcases Carrying cups of coffee and soda

Men laughing Men shouting Men gesturing with their hands

Men in the conference room Men blocking entryways Men at the refrigerator

letting the door hang open

                    Men took their time

One cornered me in the file closet and said *oh you know you want it*

One said *hey get me a coffee* and when I glared at him he said

I forgot there was a war against men

One said *ni hao wonton soup egg foo young*

One said *no tickee no shirtee*

One said *want to take you shopping for a two-piece*

One said *come with me on my boat*

One said *I'll bet you're great in the sack*

Another one agreed

One told me he had been to Korea Said *you don't know how good you've got it here*

He shook his head at me then turned away

They don't treat women so good there, he said

ARROW

One night I drove the streets   of an unfamiliar city   to wait in the lobby of a hotel
for hours   I did not know what would happen when he arrived   So much time
passed that I left   but then he called so I went back   We went to his room   I
wanted to take something   that belonged to him   to break it

Later I dreamed he was the brother   I had never known   that he had come to the
city   to give me something   that belonged to our father   he had a cardboard
box   said he was sorry   that he hadn't come sooner   My hatred for him burned
so hot   it could be confused with love

In the dream he kept asking   *What do you remember?*   he sat on the swiveling desk
chair   and I perched   on the edge of the bed   *I remember turkeys strutting*   he
took off his shoes   *in a fenced-in yard*   we could have been in any   city in the
world   *Water in a tin basin*

and our reflections   took small bottles   from the minibar and opened them   one
after the other   *floating there like plastic boats*   unwrapped bars of chocolate
Tripping over his shadow   and left them on the coffee table uneaten   *as he darted*
between mulberry trees   *an old blue bicycle*

too big for me but he ran alongside me as I rode   When he reached for me   I was already
in another place   *sweet persimmon by the spoonful*   another time   did not feel his
weight on me   *sticky on our faces*   did not feel his mouth   or his hands   *dragging*
bows and arrows

to the field behind the schoolhouse   I said   you know you will have to pay   for all
this   *watermelons set up like targets*   *on the rocks*   he said   quiet   now
concentrate   quiet   now look at me   *aim for the center*   stay with me   as
hard as you can   now now
let go—

48

CENTO FOR SEMIRAMIS / SEMIRAMIS
IF I REMEMBER

Composed of lines from Semiramis If I Remember, Keith Waldrop

I.

we build ourselves
second grade? third?

the house is lost
characters die

desolate places
flesh in pain

it is night
I do not wish to go there

I study to be useless
there is nothing harder

he tried
to bring it all back

II.

no matter how patiently unearthed

the city is doomed to disappear again

her joy, her monument

always reckoned as a wonder

no certainty

death from ideas

the city may be rebuilt

overstepping the logical year

perhaps a passion for ruins

we are given to believe there was no morning

III.

against madness, against sickness
the scab that runs the body through

unexpected occurrences
an incantation omitted

stories not yet come to light
doves bury these in their nests

IV.

all of a sudden, I was unsure
populations that live in the dark

how can we make out the detail
rough terrain, rough music

history legible, and the mess behind history
rivers deviate from their courses

the problem of meaningful, the problem
of future desires satisfied

V.

what I hear whispered, I whisper to you

some obstruction divides thought from remembrance

so much that we know, we know from tombs

then I heard, with a shock, my own voice

too late to call back on its own

VI.

Having driven ghosts from the graveyard, I haunt the graves myself

dead center
dead point
dead faint

Semiramis, impassive, gazing

the world begins in winter

THE FISH & THE DOVE: SEMIRAMIS CYCLE

The queen takes the throne by force

Ambition makes her beautiful—

her sweat-soaked gown.

Blood

on the tip of every sword.

Usurper

Pretender

Imposter

The men whisper and hiss at her but she

has their eyes plucked out

gathers them up in her skirts the way she carried

blueberries to her father as a child.

Later at the altar she lays the silver bowl down

washes her hands in a basin of holy water

then tips it out on the stone floor

orders the sightless men to their knees

to lap the water up.

Defiling something is one way to make it yours.

It is said that when she was young she licked

all the ripest fruits laid out on the table—

and who would dare touch them after that?

Semiramis was someone to write operas about.

Imagine a woman wielding power!

Imagine a woman on the ancient throne!

Beautiful and ruthless! *If we are going to be ruled by a woman,*

at least let her be a whore.

It turns them on to think of her.

The historians, I mean.

Year after year

one bloody battle after another. But what's this?

A sexy lady coming down

the annals of time?

Is she beautiful?

Yes.

Is she wicked?

Yes.

Will she punish us for our wickedness?

Yes. Baby, oh yes.

Power fits her differently than the men who came before

she wraps herself in the blood-soaked garments

prances around

but all the blood in the ocean will not bring her mother back.

Semiramis stands barefoot in the throne room trembling.

She weeps now for the sightless men, weeps

for her own father, his skin blackening where it was hung

on a pillar at the entrance to the city.

She has had vengeance. Has seen the children of her enemies

boiled and burned, their splintered bones clogging the canals.

But all the rotting skins

all the choked breath of her enemies

all the white ash littering the streets

will not bring her father back.

Has she been betrayed?

Yes, she has been betrayed.

Has she been cheated?

Yes, she has been cheated.

Does she wish to rise from the ash of her dead parents and strike down every last

living thing until it is only her own ragged breath she hears in the stillness?

Yes, she wants that, too.

Ways to Make Something Yours (working list):

> 1. Trap it.
> 2. Seduce it.
> 3. Love it.
> 4. Feed it.
> 5. Enslave it.
> 6. Name it.
> 7. Hide it.

8. Make it promises.
9. Defile it.
10. Kill it.

Men claim she is not fit for the throne. That her heart at times has been

too tender. This is not a conviction widely held.

Does she fear death?

She does.

Does she fear love?

Do not cross her.

Respect and admiration are not the same as fear

though their effects look the same in certain lights.

Standing where powerful men have stood before

is powerful—

clawing at the palace draperies with your own unwashed hands.

If at the point of your spear, men cultivate land for you

is the land yours?

If it is their blood that soaks the earth but by your hand that they bleed

does the earth too become yours?

Her father slain, her mother left

to throw herself to the sea.

They say she killed a thousand men

they say she loved a thousand more

straddled and rode them to the gated walls of the city

urged them all in—

Is love not a kind of battle

is battle not a strike of love

If you can't control it, kill it,

she has been known to say.

Some say she slayed them all,

so that none would mistake

her body's hunger for more than what it was—

A woman cannot afford affection when she has an empire to run.

Don't say you have never used another for your pleasure.

Don't say you have never wished it had all gone another way.

WOMAN'S RULE OR BOOK OF WAR

I.

Consider Semiramis

They give her a chapter in their history books—

call it "Woman's Rule"

but manage to make it about men

… yet it was his fate to marry a princess …

… such fame as was hers was due to the premature death of her husband …

… conquests attributed to Semiramis are indeed exaggerations of those which must be assigned to her period of rule …

What is a woman for, if not to feed the imaginations of men?

… the most beautiful, most cruel, most powerful, and most lustful of all the Oriental queens…

In the end, they say she is betrayed by a son

to be the mother of men is to harbor the enemy

Must a woman must always choose? Ambition or love

Love or war

II.

My father never spoke of it

but it was spoken

whispered around him *not the same after the war*

not the same

later a photograph of corpses

a photograph of fires burning

the photograph of my father's silence

hung on every wall

III.

Police action
Limited war
Civil war
Unknown war
Forgotten war

How easy it is to get into war
how unspeakable to get out

"a sudden white flash filled the corridor with light"

IV.

Found on a tree branch
Found in a trash can
Found in a basket floating to the sea

War forges its orphans
then marches in to rescue

Mongrel
Half-breed

War hammers itself out
on the bodies of women

They say her mother was a whore they say her mother

What she needs is

What she needs is

good old American

V.

Isn't girlhood in America a life-threatening condition

all the fields you skip through are laced with broken glass

girl next door who keeps the front gate open

always visible

always knowable

to be entered

They didn't call me angry but I was

They didn't call me desperate but I was

Didn't I paint my eyelids blue and try for them

gold hoop earrings big as fists

dancing at the clubs we snuck into

woozy with blackberry brandy

hips swaying all night

all wide all open

VI.

My American father leaves us to start a new life

Later he sends letters in which he tells me

about his wife

… she's just a doll …

… and she can cook …

… and let me tell you what she can do …

I tell him about a man I love

he sends a postcard back

… you tell him that I have a gun and I swear to god if he lays a hand on you …

Has it always been the same

to them in love and violence

VII.

I have collected more words than I thought possible

I read the history books but all I find is

> *perpetual war*
> *state of alert*
> *perpetual fear*

walk quickly in the dark

keep your eyes down

don't get yourself pregnant

don't get yourself raped

cross the street

tug your skirt down

stay alert

count your steps

cover your face

hold your breath

when a man says *I am walking behind you but*

I am not a threat

doesn't it just remind you

of how easily he could gut you

> *post war*
> *post mortem*
> *post meaning*

what is taken remains lost

what is lost remains lost

VIII.

In the end he says
it feels like I am burning

He tells me of the man
who died in his arms

and of the other one who tripped
on a mine

He says I looked up and there he was
raining down on me

CENTO FOR TRUTH & RECONCILIATION

*Composed of lines from the 2009 Report of the Truth & Reconciliation Commission,
Republic of Korea*

hidden and distorted for decades

onsite examinations and field surveys
unearthing the remains

differences only in the perpetrators and the pattern
strict selection criteria

cases of
corporal damage, property damage, deaths in battles
forced arrest and deaths after disappearance
murder, kidnapping
forced drafting and border-crossing
were dismissed

killings that occurred accidentally and randomly before and after
accidental bombings and general deaths caused by accidents during
        military and police operations
statements by eyewitnesses, depositions by witnesses unrelated

witnesses are categorized
according to what they witnessed
for example
the arrest
the incident or sacrifice
the collection of bodies
or the burial of bodies
executed in the front yard and buried

slain at a local brewery
lynched and killed and buried in a nearby hillock
buried in a nearby hill

selected families bound and dragged to a nearby shore

using knives, clubs, bamboo spears, and farm implements
bound with straw ropes

pushing them off a cliff near the shore
pushing them into a deep well

locked in the warehouse of the registry office and burned to death

all members of the family including the children

killed indiscriminately including babies
killed in the mountain areas near the prison
killed inside the prison
killed under the Seomun Bridge
killed in Sanseong-ri Cave

killed after failing to report to their meeting
killed after arriving late to roll call
killed for supplying food

killed after being severely tortured
killed or wounded by aircraft strafing

arranged in a line with their hands bound
summarily executed or buried alive

no power to punish perpetrators

but recommend that the government

offer official apology
provide peace and human rights education
for the police
and support memorial services
on behalf of all victims

IN THE PERMANENT COLLECTION

"Of all the crimes committed by colonizers and their ilk, this is, perhaps, one of the most insidious: condemning the descendants of their victims to a strange reality, one in which they must employ magical thinking – a personal and collective mythos —to better understand their forcible eradicated histories."

—Monica Uszerowicz

"In Korea, all arts suffered badly from centuries of invasion and warfare."
—from *East Asian Lacquers in the Collection of the Seattle Art Museum, 1992*

I. Self-Guided Tour

You call it a gallery but what I see is a tomb
all around me death's stillness, its hushed stagnant air

Collecting and mounting are ways to feel powerful
Interpreting an object is a way to make it yours

Show me where you keep the instruments of war
how you revere them

Lift the glass cases with your gloved hands
and show me the blood-burnished iron and steel

I keep company with ghosts, prefer the dead to the living
grief the cave of wonders I've walled myself in

II. Recent Acquisitions

Most of what you see here has been excavated from tombs or other archaeological sites and has been damaged during burial and exhumation and removed from its cultural context, preventing accurate provenance. Note the decorative effects marked by centuries of repeated invasion.

acres in the Geoje Region - Verified on November 25, 2008
Commission found that from March to May 1949, at least 38 people were massacred by South
an soldiers and police after being accused of collaborating with North Korean soldiers
Commission conducted interviews with perpetrators, survivors, and witnesses and reviewe
ous relevant records in order to verify the facts.

Commission found that before the executions occurred, the victims were beaten and torture
he perpetrators. Some of the victims were publicly executed in front of other villagers
as also reported that the perpetrators killed innocent family members of suspects and ex
ed individuals with the same name without properly verifying their identities.

Commission identified 38 victims, although it is assumed that the number of victims i
er. Thirty-five out of 38 of the victims' ages ranged from 20 to 30 years old, and th
ning three victims were women or in their teens. Most of the victims were either farmer
shermen who provided food and assistance to red guerillas under the threat of death. Re
less of the villagers' predicament, the perpetrators accused them of collaborating with
unists and proceeded to torture and execute the victims. The Commission recommended tha
overnment offer an official apology, provide peace and human rights education to soldiers,
e officers, and civil servants, and support memorial services on behalf of the victims.

gju Massacres - Verified on November 25, 2008
Commission found that from February 1949 to October 1951, South Korean police illegally
acred dozens   llaborating with
unists. In c   police and army
ds as well

Gwangju civi   e treated by the
ce as either   **Man's Shoe,** ca. 1951   ed based on such
sations. Som   Artist Unknown, Korean   mmunist collabo
rs killed af   social gathering
ed after bei   police and army
ysically dis   Hemp; interlaced, knotted.   eople killed for
lying food t   lled after being
sed of commu   Object Number: 2014.B5.1109
               Gift of Anonymous Donor

Commission i   olice based their
ification for   than following
er judicial

Commission r   rovide peace and
a rights edu   f of the victims

agwon Bodo League Incidents - Verified on November 4, 2008
Commission found that from early to mid July 1950, South Korean police and the Counter-in
igence Corps (CIC) massacred members of the Bodo League in the Cheongwon region. Beginnin
ate June 1950, the police imprisoned Bodo League members throughout the Cheongwon region
. in the following month, the imprisoned members were executed at over eight differen
s. In relation to these incidents, the Commission reviewed various reports and conducte
lte investigations. During the massacres, at least 232 civilians were killed, but the
ission could only identify 165 victims.

identified victims' age ranged from 20 to 30 years old. In Cheongwon County, the Commission
med 332 remains, 235 bullets, and 300 other victim-related articles. At the time of the
nation, the victims' were found to have been arranged in a line with their hands bound an
ed to kneel. Some remains showed bullet holes or fragments.

uly 10, 1950, a victim managed to survive the incident. She was present at the killing
 with her husband and other Bodo League members before being shot by South Korean sol
s. While the others died, she only lost consciousness. The Commission recommended that the
anment offer an official apology; provide peace and human rights education for soldiers,
ce, and civil servants; support memorial services on behalf of the victims, amend the
ly Registry, and provide permanent facilities to preserve the victims' exhumed remains.

Massacre at Yeongdeok, Jipum-myeon - Verified on November 4, 2008
The Commission found that from December 1949 to January 1950, South Korean soldiers exec
unarmed civilians without due process at Yoengdeok Jipum-myeon. The Commission reviewed v
ous reports, including the Special Committee Report of the National Assembly on massacres
the G-2 Periodic Report of the Korean Military Advisory Group of the US Army, and condu
on-site investigations and acquired testimonies from petitioners and reference witnesses

The Commission concluded that between December 1949 and January 1950, South Korean sol
tortured and killed civilians en masse based on the suspicions that they were collabora
with communist guerillas in the region. The Commission identified at least 34 victims and f
that the majority of them were farmers and their ages ranged from 20 to 40 years old. Co
list partisans forced the civilians to supply food which may have lead South Korean sol
to assume that they were collaborators rather than victims of coercion. However, instea
formally charging the civilians, the soldiers responded with executions.

The Commission recommended that the government offer an official apology, provide peace
human rights education to police and civil servants, and support memorial services on be
of the victims.

The Massacres at Naju Dado-myeon - Verified on October 21, 2008
The Commission found that from July 1950 to May 1951, in Naju Dado-myeon, South Korean sol
indiscriminately killed innocent civilians while subduing red guerrillas. The Commission
fied the identit   children and
elderly.

According to a d   led 'commun
while engaged i   erences howe
the soldiers an   **Tobacco Pipe**, 1951   d all avail
information and   Artist Unknown, Korean   e indeed ki
innocent civilia   res still su
from psychologic   that the gov
ment offer an of   Bamboo.   nent the fin
in historical re   strengthen p
and human rights
                        Object Number: 2016.C45.38
The Massacres in   Museum Purchase with Funds from Anonymous Donor
The Commission v   diers and po
ignored proper   on region w
subduing Red gue   and perpetra
of the massacre.   Defense and
Headquarters.

By reviewing Korean War records of the Army Headquarters, the Commission found that accom
to these reports, South Korean soldiers were involved in subduing Red guerrillas in the Na
region from the end of 1950 to the beginning of 1951. After having heard the statement
the survivors and witnesses however, the Commission confirmed that most of those killed
actually innocent civilians rather than Red guerrillas.
The Commission verified that the South Korean soldiers and police indiscriminately killed
nocent civilians, including women, children, and the elderly. It identified 90 victims.
Commission recommended that the government offer an official apology, provide support for
morial work, and promote peace and human rights education for soldiers and police.

The Massacres at Gimpo - Verified on October 7, 2008
The Commission verified that from September 28, 1950, to January 4, 1951, Gimpo residents
accused of collaborating with communists before being massacred by the South Korean pol
The commission estimated that during this period the police killed more than 600 civili
including women and children, but the Commission was only able to identify 110 victims.
commission recommended that the government offer an official apology, provide support for m
rial work, promote peace and human rights education, and take relevant measures to permane
preserve the remains of victims by giving them a proper burial and honoring their memory

The Massacres at Haenam County - Verified on July 8, 2008

hundred twenty-three petitioners filed for truth verification for several massacres con
ed by the South Korean police and right-wing groups in Haenam County from August 15, 194
he Korean War period (1950-1953). The petitioners claimed that the victims were accuse
eing communists or communist collaborators, which led to their execution without trial
Commission verified that 159 innocent civilians were killed by the South Korean police an
t-wing groups. The commission recommended that the government offer an apology, conduc
cial services for the victims, amend the relevant records, and promote peace and huma
is education.

Massacres at Cheongdo - Verified on July 8, 2008
cy-eight petitioners filed for truth verification for several massacres conducted by Sout
an soldiers at the Cheongdo and Gyeongsan cobalt mines from February 1949 to Februar
. The Commission verified that 132 civilians were killed.

e Massacre after the Yeosun Incident - Verified on July 8, 2008
Commission ascertained that between late October 1948 and July 1949 in Gurye, shortl

c the Yeo	lled and sac
ed as Sou	o subdue com
st rebell	separate fro
Yeosun In	

Girl's Locket, 1951
Artist Unknown

oximately	ere identifie
r going c	s, Historica
rds of Su	rs (1954) an
ements fr	

This heart-shaped locket is hung on a delicate
gold chain. Its size and the length of its chain
suggest it belonged to a young girl. The locket
is empty, although it appears it may once have
contained a small photograph. If you look closely,
you will see that the chain has been broken, sug-
gesting the locket might have been torn away or
taken forcefully.

Object Number: 2016.X5.09
Museum Purchase with Funds from Anonymous Donor

South Kor	lians accuse
ollaborat	that village
ted near	aboration be
being ex	ries of thes
killings	the 1st an
Battalion	egion.
e Police	munist parti
and comm	their bodie
earby are	tion in Gurye
directly	by providin
times gro	filiated wit
unist gue	

Korean Yo	lal of bodie
c the exe	ege that the

im joined a left-leaning organization such as the Socialist Labor Party in South Korea
c accusations that resulted in death were as minor as the victim having resided near area
eted by the military or being related to suspected victims.
South Korean troops and police forces commonly conducted indiscriminate arrests, deten
, or imprisonment. They also tortured and summarily executed people without adequate con
tion procedures or legitimate judicial processes. The proclaimed martial law at the tim
not supported by any legality, and thus the administrative and judicial authorities of the
t commander under martial law were subject to revocation.

hermore, the administrative and judicial authority given during the proclaimed martial la
arbitrarily interpreted and implemented by regional chiefs, thereby increasing the numbe
ivilian casualties. Even if the martial law were legitimate, the principle of non-combat
immunity was often neglected.
etrators often practiced a type of extra-judicial punishment in conducting summary exe
ons. This was often misunderstood to be a given right that allowed them to arbitraril
civilians. Even with

martial law, summary executions should abide by military regulations. Thus, massacres b▮ ▮outh's authorities could not be justified in any way.

▮he Commission found that the killing of innocent civilians by the public authorities in ▮ ▮nd Suncheon greatly transgressed the constitutional legality given to the military and p▮ ▮orce at the time. They failed their sacred obligations of protecting the lives and pro▮ ▮f civilians. Hereby, the Commission advised the government to officially apologize to th▮ ▮eaved families of the victims, restore the honor of the dead, revise the historical re▮ ▮n accordance with the findings, and reinforce education on sustaining peace.

▮anghwa Case of Civilian Executions - July 8, 2008
▮he Commission concluded that the Ganghwa Regional Self-defense Forces accused and kille▮ ▮ivilians residing in the Ganghwa, Seokmo, and Jumun island areas around the time of the ▮ary 4, 1951 retreat (1.4 Retreat). Details of the executions began to surface when a ▮ ▮f residents in Ganghwa registered their deceased family members as victims under the K▮ ▮ar Veteran Memorial Law. During the registration period, details about the victims, as ▮s perpetrators, emerged and revealed enough information to speculate the circumstances ▮ounding the incident.

▮t the time of the massacre, the Ganghwa Regional Self-defense Forces assumed that if ▮

▮orean troops o▮▮   r families ▮
▮ollaborate with   ▮as thought ▮
▮ strategically ▮   ▮ in 12 diff▮
▮ownships in the   ▮ns adminis▮
▮fter the 1.4 Re▮   ▮m the South
▮ean and U.S. fo

20 Bullets from M1 Carbine, ca. 1950
Artist Unknown

Recovered from excavation site in Bongseong
Mt. Cemetery in Gurye-gun, South Jeolla
Province (Yeosu-Suncheon Incident), 2007.

Object Number: 2009.D75.09
Museum Purchase with Funds from Anonymous Donor

▮t the time of   ing intellig▮
▮n secret milita   st Coast. I▮
▮ourse of their   as the Gan▮
▮elf-defense For   ▮ summary e▮
▮ions against ci   ty. The vic▮
▮ain and sufferi   forms of s▮
▮iscrimination a

▮hile direct res   ▮ctive civil▮
▮anizations invo   government
▮lso be held acc   and contro▮
▮egional authori   f-defense F▮
▮n organization   as provided
▮y the government. The arms were then used to assault civilians. The government's acti▮ ▮iving arms allowed for the deaths of innocent villagers.
▮fter uncovering these findings, the Commission advised the government to officially apol▮ ▮o the victims' bereaved families, seek reconciliation between the victims and perpetra▮ ▮nd arrange adequate emergency alternatives considering Ganghwa's geographical circumsta▮

Uljin Massacre - Verified on June 3, 2008
▮he Commission ascertained that at least 256 civilians were killed in Uljin, Gangwon ▮ ▮nce after being accused of collaborating with local leftists. The incident occurred be▮ September 26, 1950 and late December, 1950. A total of 256 victims were identified th▮ ▮horough reviews of historical documents, testimonies from witnesses and petitioners, ▮ecords from the Uljin Police Station. Extensive field research was also conducted throu▮ ▮he region. The perpetrators were identified as the Uljin Police, CIC, and the 3rd Army ▮ ▮ion of South Korea.

▮n October 20, 1950, the 3rd Army's reserve forces searched for villagers accused as ▮ ▮eftist. They based their hunt on lists of names submitted by local right-wing organiza▮ ▮nd the village chiefs. Approximately 40 people accused of collaborating with the North, ▮ ▮ith many others scheduled for execution, were confined at the Uljin Police Station and ▮arily executed or buried alive in the Budul Valley, Hujeong-ri.

ween October and November 1950, the Uljin Police Office released some of the prisoner
sferred from subordinate police branches in the region, but approximately 250 of the re
ing prisoners were segregated for summary execution. They were killed and buried in th
 Valley, Shinrim. On November 26, 1950, officers from the Onjeong Police Branch shot an
ed 12 captives en route to the Uljin Police Office.

the late fall of 1950, several local villagers were indicted of offering food to thei
tives who were seeking refuge after having been accused of treachery. The villagers wer
uted in a valley in Sagye-ri, Buk-myeon by officers from the Hadang Police Branch. Accord
to the Commission, a total of 256 identified victims, including many innocent civilians
 massacred in a series of mass killings conducted by the 3rd Army's reserve forces and th
h Korean local police forces. The victimized villagers were blamed for holding certai
tions during North Korea's occupation over the region or for registering with organiza
s considered traitorous.

ver, most
 summaril
nts, many
he North
ntarily j
agers wer

e summary
e a crime
heir desc
vering su
aved fami
ices for

 Force's
y-three p
ing Incid
g Provinc
e were no
Force bom
scape fro
its of th
 governme
Bombing o

anuary 3,
 Army, Li
lock refu

Girl's School Uniform, 1952
Artist Unknown

Here we see a typical outfit for a young girl in
Korea, consisting of a blue skirt and white blouse,
both made from a cotton weave textile common
for the day. The pleated style of the skirt and the
rounded collar of the blouse indicate a school
uniform, possibly for a girl of thirteen or fourteen
years of age. Note the hand-stitching on the hem,
which indicates repeated mending. The uneven
stitching suggests the mending might have been
done hastily.

Object Number: 2016.Y7.112
Gift of Anonymous Donor

tims' charge
ne of the in
ed the borde
sively or in
i cases wher

dered by man
y passed dow
judice. Afte
logize to th
nold memoria

. Air Force'
North Chungc
. Even thoug
ers, the U.S
as they trie
ement of th
he Korean an
fugee Contro

eeting of 8t
and IX Corp
ilians ignor

the refugee control order and to request air strikes. Lieutenant General Ridgeway the
rmed the South Korean army of this decision.

to the use of the representative coordinates on Mosquito Mission Reports (MMR) however
tailed record regarding the bombing of the cave was never recorded, but on the U.S. Arm
Journals and S-3 Journals of January 20, the attack had been clearly stated. Most peopl
he cave suffered burns and suffocated to death due to the use of napalm bombs. Others
barely escaped from the cave, were killed or wounded by aircraft strafing. Although th
itnesses testified that the U.S. forces visited the cave and investigated the results o
bombing and mass civilian victimization, no follow-up measures were taken. * Numbers an
acteristics of Victims and Responsibility of the U.S. Army

total number of victims of this incident is estimated to be over 200 with 167 of the
tified. The rate of juvenile victims under the age of 19 is considerably high at 62%. Th
er of female victims exceeds the number of male victims.

his incident involved a large number of non-combatant civilians being killed by U.S. bomb
perations. Pursuant to the International Humanitarian Law, U.S. forces had violated t
esponsibilities at that time: 1 U.S. forces did not conduct any complementary measure
rotect the refugees affected by the blockade. 2 Especially knowing that there were l
umbers of refugees in the area, U.S. forces should have decided whether to bomb the cave
fter conducting proper reconnaissance verifying that the people in the cave were indeed
oldiers. 3 U.S. force's bombing operations and incinerations in the vicinity of the
nd Yongchun-myeon, Danyang-gun indicate indiscriminating bombing beyond the boundary of
peration and without proper regard for the refugees in the area.

amyangju Suspicion of Treachery Case - Verified on May 6, 2008
rom October to December 1950, police and security forces, later reorganized as the l
efense force, massacred at least 118 Jinjeop residents, including their family memb
n charges of treachery. In early October 1950, when the South Korean army reclaimed
amyangju region, Yangju and Jinjeop police officers, along with Jinjeop security police,
ained approximately 200 people, including the family members of those suspected of treac
uring the North Korean occupation. The victims were
elocated to the township office storehouse and executed.

n the middle of December 1950, shortly before the retreat of the South Korean army on J
ry 4, 1951, the   of collabora
ith the North K   a recommenda
rder from the G   retly buried
odies. This mas   before the S
Korean army retr   and the elde

ased on the mat   mates that t
ere more than 4   nted due to
f identification   ly identified
ictims. The per   e, and the l
efense force co   ans without
ence and based   with the en
he actions of t

t the end of De   s petitioned
special invest   ion team was
sembled. Compose   hey interrog
he perpetrators   i. This docu
pecifically deta   nassacre and
mmediate cover-

Yellow Cardigan, Blue Skirt, 1952
Artist Unknown, Korean

Wool, cotton. Tags have been removed, but both the cardigan and skirt show few signs of wear.

Object Number: 2010.C45.09
New Works Acquisition Fund

he special inspection team's investigation disregarded this, and instead concentrated
fforts on the testimonies of the perpetrators. Compared to the size of the case, the in
tigation was poorly conducted as evidenced by distortions in the perpetrators' motives
he victims' characteristics. As to whether the perpetrators stood trial and were punis
t remains unknown. The Commission recommends that the government officially apologize
rovide support for memorial-related projects and work, and provide human rights educa
for the general public.

he Korean National 11th Army Division in the Gochang Region Case - Verified on April 8,
he Commission's investigation results found that from December 1950 to March 1951, the Ko
lational 11th Army Division stationed in Jeonbuk Gochang region perpetrated mass execut
of civilians while searching for communist guerrillas. The Commission identified 273 vict
lthough the total number is likely higher considering that some families did not file a p
ion, or were relocated, or killed.
he first incident occurred on December 22, 1950, as refugees moved from the Dongho-ri re
to an area near the Simone-myeon Seashore. Upon encountering them, the 11th Army Divi
ndiscriminately shot and killed 200-300 refugees. Another incident occurred on Januar
1951 when the 11th Army Division, 6th Company pursued 150-200 refugees. After capturing
refugees, the soldiers bound each person with straw ropes before executing them with l
achine gunfire. A day later, the 6th Company

by shooting them in an open area next to Sangha Elementary School.

March 13th, 1951, after a scouting soldier was killed near Sangha-myeon, the 11th Arm
sion killed approximately 50 local residents while searching for communist sympathizers
he same time, near the Sangha-myeon Seashore, a group of civilians were killed by bein
scriminately fired upon by the 8th Company of the 11th Army Division.

he time, the 11th Army Division justified these types of incidents by emphasizing the dif
ty in distinguishing civilians from guerrillas. They reasoned that any dangerous threa
be eliminated and reasoned that mass executions prevented communist sympathizers fro
upting military objectives. It may have been necessary to place certain restrictions o
le considering the instability of the situation at the time. As a whole, people's basi
rties were limited in order to guard against national security threats, and society wa
rganized during the Korean army's reclamation process. On the contrary, the Korean army'
execution of unarmed and non-resisting civilians without proper due process violated bot
rnational human rights and Korea's guaranteed constitutional rights.

a nation deprives its citizens' of life, or punishes people by physically restrainin
, a nation must abide by the law and have proper reason to conduct such actions. The per
ators of
mmended t
human rig

Black Cotton Bundle Containing Underwear, Sanitary Towels & Soap, 1951
Artist Unknown, Korean

This loosely-wrapped bundle contained personal
items that a young woman might have packed
for a short journey. The cotton is rough-hewn
indicating modest means. The items appear to
have been thrown together rather than packed
neatly, and the knot in the cotton is askew,
suggesting the bundle might have been prepared
quickly.

Object Number: 2016.Y445.01
New Works Acquisition Fund

ot be justified under the principle of discrimination or the principle of proportionality

n Bodo League Massacre - Verified on November 27, 2007
hundred sixteen petitioners appealed for truth verification for several massacres, number
over ten, which occurred in Ulsan throughout August 1950. According to the petitioners
870 innocent Bodo League members were killed by South Korean police. The Commission wa
to verify the truth, but only 407 of the 870 victims were identified.

Commission recommended to the government to restore the victims' honor, offer an officia
ogy, establish memorials for the victims, and revise historical and public records t
ct the new findings. It is also recommended that the government promote peace and huma
ts education programs and amend any relevant laws.

ng Massacre Incident - Verified on November 20, 2007
petitioners appealed for truth verification for 240 civilians massacred by right-wing
ps at Goyang. These paramilitary groups, supported by the South Korean police, claime
the victims were North Korean collaborators. After conducting the investigation, the
ission found that the right-wing groups illegally arrested and killed unarmed civilians

illing of Civilians by the US Force Bombing: Sansung-dong, Yechon Bombing Incident – Ve
on November 20, 2007

he Commission ascertained that at least 51 residents were killed at Sansung-dong, Yecheo
o U.S. Air Force bombing. It is stated in official military documents dated January 19,
hat the U.S. Air Force conducted three bombings with 18 fighter-bombers, including the
4U, and AD. The fighter-bombers dropped Napalm bombs over Sansung-dong and strafed house
nhabitants in the area.

lthough at that time North Korean forces were concentrated in the vicinity of Hakga 1
ain, no enemy was present in Sansung-dong. Therefore misreading the coordinates is as
s a possible reason for the attacks. According to the Mosquito Mission Report, "many pe
n white in area of DR 6457," yet at that time, most Korean civilians wore white clo
herefore, this could be offer another explanation for the bombings against the peopl
ansung-dong.

he 'area bombing' policy for the elimination of the North Korean troops' possible shelte
his area seems to be not an indispensable strategy of military necessity. Due to these
ngs, only the innocent civilians became victims, therefore it cannot be justified unde
"Principle of Proportionality". Even according to the U.S. documents, North Korean sol
were not present at Sansung-dong.

t the time of		pursuant to
ositive law of		ustoms of Wa
and (1907) and		e Draft Rule
ir Warfare (192	**45 Caliber Handgun, Several M1 Bullets &**	agers' reco.
ions, there was	**Cartridges**, ca. 1952	e U.S. Air
violated the "Pr	Artist Unknown	
		tion" in dis
he U.S. Air For		rs. But the
guishing between	Recovered from excavation site in Golryeong-	y violated
hat the U.S. A	gol and Nangwol-dong in Daong-gu, Daejon	
rinciple of Pre	(Daejeon Penitentiary), 2007.	
		hould be pe
considerable n	Object Number: 2016.A53.01	distinguishe
specially protec	Museum Purchase with Funds from Anonymous Donor	y a bombing
ir patrols as r		military ta
arget must be s		whether an
ven if it is a		owever, the
vilians dwell in		Discriminat
ir Force conduc		

he Sancheong Massacres – Verified on November 20, 2007
ne hundred thirty-two petitioners appealed for truth verification for 129 civilians massa
y the South Korean army in Sanchong County, Gyeongsangnam Province. The petitioners cla
hat the massacres took place between July 1949 and January 1950. The Commission verified
29 civilians were massacred. The Commission recommended that the government offer an ap
y, conduct memorial services, restore the victims' honor, revise the related laws, amen
relevant records, and promote human rights education.

he Jeju Seottal Oreum Massacre Case – Verified on November 13, 2007
wo hundred seventeen petitioners appealed for truth verification for 218 civilians massa
y the South Korean Army at Seottal Oreum on Jeju Island on August 20, 1950. Almost a n
before the massacre, on July 16, 1950, the civilians were arrested and detained by the
Korean police without a specific charge. They were later formally accused of being commu
ympathizers.

he Commission verified that no evidence existed to support such a charge. The Commission
ommended to the government to restore the victims' honor, offer an official apology, estab
memorials for the victims, and revise historical and public records to reflect the new find
t is also recommended that the government promote peace and human rights education prog
and amend any relevant laws.

NOTES

By most available accounts, Semiramis (c 800 BCE) was an ancient Assyrian queen and warrior. In one of the many legends that surround her life and reign, she is said to have been the orphaned daughter of an ill-fated love between a fish goddess and a mortal man. She is said to have been raised by doves.

The poem "Legacy" owes a debt to the short story "Rabbits" by Mieko Kanai, from the 1982 collection, *Rabbits, Crabs, Etc.: Stories by Japanese Women* (translated by Phyllis Birnbaum).

"Woman's Rule" references "Chapter XIII: Woman's Rule, Approach to Monotheism, and Decline," from A.T. Olmstead's 1923 *History of Assyria*.

In 2009, the "Truth and Reconciliation: Activities of the Past Three Years," report was released by the Truth & Reconciliation Commission, Republic of Korea. Established in 2005, the Commission's purpose was to "reveal the truth behind massacres during the Korean War, human rights abuses during the authoritarian rule, the anti-Japanese independence movement, and the history of overseas Koreans."

Other sources and references include:

The Bridge at No Gun Ri: A Hidden Nightmare from the Korean War, Charles J. Hanley, Sang-Hun Choe, and Martha Mendoza, Henry Holt & Company, 2001.

The Korean War: An Oral History, Donald Knox, Harcourt Brace & Company, 1985.

Semiramis If I Remember (Self-Portrait as Mask), Keith Waldrop, Avec Books, 2001.

ACKNOWLEDGEMENTS

Poems from *The Fish & The Dove*, often in different forms, have appeared in the following publications:

"Self-Portrait as Semiramis" appeared in Poem-A-Day. Thanks to the Academy of American Poets and to Don Mee Choi, guest editor, November 2018.

An earlier version of "In The Permanent Collection" appeared online in *Tupelo Quarterly* in November 2018. Thanks to Kristina Marie Darling, Editor-in-Chief.

Earlier versions of "History" and "Occupation" appeared in *Hyperallergic* in March 2019. Thanks to Wendy Xu, Poetry Editor.

An alternate version of "In The Permanent Collection" appeared online in *Conjunctions* in March 2019. Thanks to Bradford Morrow, Editor.

Special thanks to Heidi Rezsies and Artifact Press for publishing a beautiful chapbook of a cycle of poems, *Between Night & Night*, which were part of an earlier draft of *The Fish & The Dove*.

Thanks also to Andrea Beltran and Shahira Kudsi for showcasing a version of "Self-Portrait as Semiramis" online at *Fog Machine*.

LOVE & GRATITUDE

Firstly, for everything, my thanks to Noemi Press: Carmen Giménez Smith, Suzi F. Garcia, and Sarah Gzemski.

To Xander Marro for the cover image, "Arrows" and to Steve Halle for cover design.

Thanks to Brandon Shimoda, Jordan Davis, Diana Khoi Nguyen, and Sam Roxas-Chua 姚 for their generous attention to this book and for their kind endorsements.

Special thanks to Marisa Siegel and Brian Spears for including *The Fish & The Dove* in the Rumpus Poetry Club. Marisa's support has meant a great deal to me over the years.

Thank you to David Naimon for his ongoing willingness to have a conversation about *The Fish & The Dove* for "Between the Covers." I am very much looking forward to it.

For their love and support in many ways over many years, my thanks to Paula Krebs, Laurie Bosman, Claire Buck, Jessica David, Stephen Crocker, Kate Schapira, Kate Colby, and Darcie Dennigan. Thanks to Joan Harrison.

My work would not be possible without Providence. I am fortunate to live in such a vibrant, generous, and eclectic arts community. There are so many people who have inspired, supported, and sustained me and in whose company I feel honored to live and work. Among them in no particular order: Brooke Erin Goldstein, Shey Rivera Ríos, Sara Wintz, Seth Tourjee, Amy Pickworth, Tina Cane, Sarah Ganz Blythe, Alexandra Poterack, Christina Bevilacqua, Benjamin Lundberg

Torres Sánchez, Becci Davis, Holly Ewald, Phil Eil, Janaya Kizzie, Flannery Patton, Roger Blumberg, Matt Tracy. Thanks to Matthew Lawrence and Jason Tranchida. Thanks to Deb Domody. Thanks to Xander Marro, Pippi Zornoza, and the amazing community of artists they've fostered through two decades of the Dirt Palace. Thanks to Kath Connolly and Janet Isserlis. Thanks to Lucas Mann. To Alison Espach and Eric Bennett. To Taylor Polites, Sarah Baldwin, Brian Goldberg. Thanks to Brent and Jenna Legault and Ada Books. To Yoon Soo Lee and Ziddi Misgana, Melissa Kievman and Brian Mertes.

For generous financial and professional support, my thanks to the Rhode Island Foundation, the MacColl Johnson Fellowship, and to Neil Steinberg. Thanks also to the Rhode Island State Council on the Arts (RISCA), to Randy Rosenbaum, Cristina DiChiera, and Mollie Flanagan.

For championing my work in various ways, my thanks to Mathias Svalina and Sam Ace. Thanks and love to Elizabeth Schmuhl, Melissa Matthewson, Mo Duffy Cobb, and in particular for reading earlier versions of this book, my thanks to Eric Raymond, Allison Grimaldi-Donahue, Andrea Blancas Beltran, and Lauren Banks.

For inviting me to great places to read and share my work, my thanks to Carrie Oeding, Sarah Fawn Montgomery, Selah Saterstrom, Joanna Howard, Thirii Myo Kyaw Myint, Éireann Lorsung, Jeffrey Thompson, Art Middleton, Jenny Gropp, Laura Solomon, Ann Hood, Jen McClanaghan, Thibault Raoult, Alexandra Mattraw, Karla Kelsey, Shira Dentz, Katie Rainey, Devin Gael Kelly, Brian Gresko, and Tracy Strauss. Thanks to Soham Patel, Irene Hsu, and Lauren Westerfield. Thanks to Eric LeMay. Thanks to Travis Sharp and Essay Press.

Thanks to the Fourth Kingdom, in particular and always to Jimin Han, Alexander Chee, Matthew Salesses, and R.O. Kwon. Thanks to Nicole Chung.

Thanks to all who are have been and continue to be such wonderful virtual company, in all your glittering pixels, too numerous to name. I am grateful to you.

Thanks always to the poetry teachers, in particular Jen Bervin, Mary Ruefle, Jamaal May. Thanks to Gale Nelson. Thanks to Myung Mi Kim.

With love to my family, the daSilvas, Larocchias, and the Derbys.

With love to Zooey and William.

This book is dedicated with love and admiration to Matthew Derby. With you, everything becomes possible and suffused with light.